THE TRUST CODE

UNCOVERING THE SECRET TO ORGANIZATIONAL SUCCESS

JOEY STUTSON

WITH CONTRIBUTING AUTHORS:

CHRISTOPHER DIEM
ROSCOE S. HOUSTON
DR. STEPHEN KALALUHI

The Trust Code

THE TRUST CODE:
UNCOVERING THE SECRET TO ORGANIZATIONAL SUCCESS

Copyright © 2018 by Joey Stutson

ISBN-13: 978-1986712507
ISBN-10: 1986712508

All rights reserved. No part of this book may be reproduced or transmitted in any form or by any means without written permission from the author.

Printed in the United States of America.

10 9 8 7 6 5 4 3 2 1

DEDICATION

This book is dedicated to those who are brave enough to forge their own path, resilient enough to stand stoically in the face of adversity, and daring enough to follow their dream of living life on their own terms. This book is dedicated to those who look at the challenge of breaking with the status quo, and instead of cowering before it, say to themselves, "Is that all you got?" This book is dedicated to those who believe in themselves, those who believe they can build the life they desire, those who believe that success is on the other side of fear. This book is dedicated to those who have chosen to rise to the occasion, rise to the challenge, and rise to the great calling they have on their lives.

The Trust Code

TABLE OF CONTENTS

INTRODUCTION	15
TRUST – A TRIANGLE OF PRACTICES AND IDEAS	21
STRENGTH IN NUMBERS	49
THE POWER OF THE DETOUR	87
ORGANIZATIONAL LIFEBLOOD	105
FINAL THOUGHTS AND INSPIRATION	123
MEET THE AUTHORS	127

Uncovering the Secret to Organizational Success

JOEY ACKNOWLEDGES

I want to acknowledge Dr. Stephen Kalaluhi for providing legendary service, and inspirational vision to gather, build and launch visionary leaders to implement their talents by collaborating. Your vision and implementation is a representation of John Maxwell's Leadership Law of the Lid.

To my bride, soul mate and best friend Allie. With you, I can scale a mountain and become the leader God wants me to become. Thank you for being courageously beautiful. Your dreams, gifts, talents, and abilities are far above my own. Thank you for always believing the best is yet to come.

To the greatest team of people and leaders at The Ken Blanchard Companies. Thank you for modeling servant leadership. I believe we will reach 10 million more lives by 2020.

CHRIS ACKNOWLEDGES

First and foremost, I want to thank my wonderful wife, Rochelle, for her encouragement and patience in the pursuit of my goals and dreams. Without her, I would not be where I am today. I want to thank my parents, Sandra and Wrex, for their support in virtually every venture I've entered over my life. I want to thank my sister, Lisa, and brother, Brian. I have had good examples to follow. I spent most of my adult life as a Marine and there are two leaders I want to thank personally for their leadership, guidance, and counsel during my career: Colonel Barry Cronin, retired, and Chief Warrant Officer 4 Michael Rhodes, retired. You both gave me a chance to do something more and have been a shining example of great leadership. I took many lessons from many Marines, but yours always ring. Lastly, I want to thank you for trusting me to share these ideas and concepts with you. There are a lot of books, trainings, and teachings on this subject and I am appreciative of your trust in me. It is my hope each of you will take something from this book and make a positive change in the world.

ROSCOE ACKNOWLEDGES

To my wife and kids: Thank you so much for your support and commitment to allow me the time, and space to peacefully complete this. I'm forever thankful for you and love you all dearly.

I would like to thank my mentors, Matt Eventoff of Princeton Public Speaking, and Joseph Jingoli of Joseph Jingoli Construction. You both are the light at the end every tunnel I've ever found myself in. Having you both in my life exposed me to greatness! Thank you for modeling great leadership, and cultivating great working atmospheres to thrive in!

I also want to give my appreciation to Dr. Stephen Kalaluhi of StephenK Leadership for being a great visionary and overseer for this project! Being a part of this has accelerated my vision to impact and serve the marketplace with excellence.

STEPHEN ACKNOWLEDGES

First and foremost, I want to thank God for giving me the strength to be the husband, father, and business owner that I currently am. Without His grace and favor, I would not be the man I am today. I must also give thanks to my beautiful bride of 24 years, also known as 1/3 of my Why. Without her support, prayers, patience, and occasional kick in the pants, my coaching practice would not have gotten off the ground. The other 2/3 of my Why (also known as my two sons) represent my heart and my soul. These two young men drive me to want to be better, not for myself, but to show them that there is better out there if they are willing to put in the time, effort, and energy to make it so. Last but not least, I want to thank you for your trust in me. There are tons of books on the subject of building trust within organizations, but the fact you are reading this makes me want to create the very best book I possibly can.

INTRODUCTION

The book that you now hold in your hands is the culmination of years of organizational experience as it pertains to trust. Many books have been written on the idea of trust, and many authors have attempted to write on those secrets they believed were key to uncovering the success of an organization.

What sets this book apart from every other book on the shelf is the real-life stories shared by these authors. Stories of surviving organizations that had little to no trust. Stories of being in the trenches and coming out the other side bigger, better, stronger, and faster.

The insight contained within these pages will accelerate your growth as a leader, but more importantly, it will accelerate the process that creates and builds trust in you and your team.

At the end of the day, the only thing worth worrying about isn't how much growth you're experiencing as a leader, or how much success you perceive as attaining. No, the only thing worth worrying about at the end of the day is whether you trust your team, and whether your team trusts you.

Because where there is no trust, success is just a fleeting concept, at best.

The stories shared with you in this book are designed to show you you're not alone in the struggles faced with building and enhancing trust. If we're being honest with ourselves (and I'm not sure why we wouldn't be), every leader in every organization on the face of the planet suffers from this challenge.

What separates you, however, is you chose to pick up this book. You chose to learn how to uncover the secret to organizational success. You chose to tap into the Trust Code.

And because of this one act, I know you will be successful. So here's to your continued growth and success!

Uncovering the Secret to Organizational Success

CHAPTER 1

Uncovering the Secret to Organizational Success

IF PEOPLE LIKE YOU, THEY'LL LISTEN TO YOU. IF THEY TRUST YOU, THEY'LL DO BUSINESS WITH YOU.

- Zig Ziglar

Uncovering the Secret to Organizational Success

TRUST – A TRIANGLE OF PRACTICES AND IDEAS

- by Christopher Diem

What is Trust?

Trust is belief, plain and simple…good or bad. Once the belief exists, trust becomes the foundation; whether it be a foundation of stone or sand. Trust is truly the determining factor of success or failure in any organization and/or relationship. There are a lot of ideas and beliefs out there about trust, and definitions, too. But for me, trust boils down to a couple of key factors. The factors include, but are not limited to, integrity, consistency, and accountability (the Trust Triangle). These three factors are the foundation of looking at how trust is either a contributor or detractor from success in an organization.

I think INTEGRITY is the most important piece to any relationship. It flows along a two-way street and must be a focus of attention for everyone involved. In its simplest form, integrity is doing the right thing (always) even when the right thing is not the easiest thing to do.

It's following the path of the moral compass, especially if no one else is looking at what one is doing. Integrity is also one of those unique things in the world where you must make a conscious decision to give up your integrity. Once you abdicate integrity, it is very hard to earn back the TRUST of people.

CONSISTENCY is high on my list of key factors because practicing consistency helps build trust between people and within organizations or destroys trust between people and within organizations.

If the consistency possesses positive and ethical influence, then everything is built upon a strong foundation. This can include following through on promises, always being there, on time and with tasks completed, and even just being available to hear other points of view and ideas. However, when people cannot rely on you to "get things done" or "be there for them," negativity grows and problems thrive. So, again, just like integrity, consistency ties directly into TRUST.

Then we move into the world of ACCOUNTABILITY. Again, accountability encompasses both positive and negative realms concerning trust. Accountability means holding yourself accountable (integrity) for accomplishing the mission and continually doing it (consistency). It also plays a strong role in holding others to strong standards and accomplishments. But, just like everything else, there is another side to the accountability coin.

Failing to hold yourself accountable and others accountable for actions or inactions embraces negativity and breaks down the foundations of trust. Advancing and growing just cannot happen when accountability doesn't exist. Following along the lines integrity and consistency, accountability rounds out the TRUST triangle for strong organizational culture.

If trust does not exist, amazing things are not likely to happen or be achieved. If trust does exist, the possibilities of greatness are virtually limitless. This is why building a strong level of trust within an organization is paramount to success – or failing to do so is a tremendous contributor to failure.

AN EXAMPLE OF TRUST TRANSITION

**** THE BAD ****

I am reminded of a story from an office in the military where trust went through an extreme transition. You see, the military is one of the rare places where leadership can completely change in a few days. Although this is not usually ideal, there are times where this type of leadership change has powerfully positive results.

THE STORY OF FRANK AND TOM

Frank was the big boss in the office and Tom was second in command. However, there should be a relationship of coexistence where Frank can ask Tom for guidance and Tom can ask Frank for guidance. This back and forth, exchange of ideas and input, did not come to fruition. Egos got in the way of leading and trusting.

There existed a HUGE problem between them. Frank did not like Tom and Tom did not like Frank. Why did this matter for trust? Because if there is no trust, leadership cannot occur. Tom cannot be led and Frank cannot lead.

This dynamic would not matter very much if the only people in the office were Frank and Tom. They could do their own things and not worry about the other person. Disdain and egos could rule the day and no one would really suffer. But this is an office with more than just Frank and Tom working there.

The relationship between Frank and Tom was bad enough for them, but the real victims of their pettiness were their subordinates…the young men and women looking to be led by them. Their overinflated sense of self and hatred (this is the best word to describe how they felt about each other) had a negative impact on the entire office staff.

- So, you may be asking why "hatred" is the right word. I understand. Just to give you some insight to things, I will share their parting story with you. The military has a tradition of "going away celebrations" when people leave an office, especially the leadership. Well, at their going away, things became quite heated between Frank and Tom in language and almost escalated to a physical altercation. If it were not for cooler heads prevailing, both would have likely ended up going to jail for assault and battery.

Believe it or not, the military often has timelines and deadlines for completing tasks. This was no different in the office. Generally, paperwork for assignments were due every 30 days. However, due to the problems in trust between the leaders, all of the paperwork was between 30 and 90 days late in being submitted.

So, the question has to be asked, "Who was to blame for the late work?" I submit the fault sat squarely on the shoulders of Frank and Tom. The "worker-bees" did not do the work because they were not held accountable for late work. Add to this, the fact egos prevailed at the leadership level and things changed every other day, it is no doubt work did not get accomplished.

Here's an example –

- If Frank said the sky is blue and the grass is green – Tom would say the sky is purple and the grass is orange.
- If Frank said to complete tasks sequentially (A then B then C, etc.) – Tom would say start with Q then move to L then go to A, etc.

This inconsistency in how to do things and what to believe left everyone unsure of how or what to do. Leading to the widely understood concept – CONFUSED PEOPLE TAKE NO ACTION! And this office was completely filled with confused people. The lack of consistency (or the consistency of being inconsistent) funneled directly into no one holding themselves accountable or anyone else accountable.

And if consistency and accountability did not exist, integrity was the third leg missing. No one followed a moral compass...no one did the right thing for the sake of doing the right thing. Thus, trust in leadership, trust in the organization, and trust in each other did not exist. This is what happens to an organization's culture when trust is dead.

One last important and contributing factor to organizational failure – Frank and Tom did not really lead or want to lead. They wanted to do the work, not really supervise the workers. I have seen this in other organizations and each time it exists, failure is the only result. No one grows; no one learns; no one has the chance to succeed.

**** THE GOOD ****

How could a complete failure of an organization turn things around and succeed? The answer is simple…TRUST! You see, Frank and Tom left the organization at the same time and new leadership took the reins. Usually, when new leadership takes control, there is a period of assessing people, activities, and culture.

However, things were in such disarray, drastic and immediate action had to be taken. The ship had to be righted, and quickly. Now, the transition was not without difficulty and turmoil. Challenges to the new leadership did happen; however, swift action squashed them quickly.

Uncovering the Secret to Organizational Success

The organization's Trust Triangle had to be rebuilt. The three key pieces to the triangle remained Integrity, Consistency, and Accountability. Just as these pieces tied together in the failure of the organization, they would equally intertwine in its success.

THE WAY IT SHOULD HAPPEN

When a transition of bosses (leadership) takes place, the old bosses should bring the new boss up to speed and get them familiar with the happenings of the office. Then, the new boss should take a few weeks, or even up to a month, to evaluate the situations, his or her people, and the flow of how work activities are accomplished. This makes sense and will generally lessen the turmoil caused by change.

As we all know, change is constant and it is the most difficult part of life in an office. No one likes for things to change too drastically or too quickly. Unfortunately for Mike and his new office, a drastic and quick change of things was required. A smooth transition was not in the cards for anyone.

THE STORY OF MIKE

Mike faced huge problems and dilemmas in his new office. The ability to assess through a transition did not exist. Change had to come quick and he knew it would be painful for all involved.

The outgoing bosses left a mess where trust was non-existent and the trust triangle was completely broken on all sides – integrity / accountability / consistency. The only good thing Mike could see in front of him was the fact he knew tremendous change had to take place and problems were abundant.

Mike knew the trust triangle had to be rebuilt and established quickly. So, he identified the biggest problem and tackled the various parts of the problem simultaneously. It may sound strange, but because each problem within the biggest problem tied to together, fixing them as individual problems and as a group of problems all at once actually worked quite well.

The biggest problem involved reports. The pieces to the biggest problem were the reports were late, incomplete, and poorly written.

Reports were due for review on a 30-day basis. Therefore, not every report was late. Some had been started within the previous 30-days. These became the priority for completion. The current reports could not fall into the late report category. People had to work quickly to ensure they did not get submitted late.

The reports only "a little" late would be tackled next. Completing the task of getting all reports up to date had to follow a logical path. And Mike decided stuff really late could wait because it was already too late. Eventually, this method would allow for all the reports to be completed and put the office on a path to getting things done on time.

REBUILDING THE TRUST TRIANGLE

Mike decided to implement some immediate changes to how business was done in the office. First, Mike is a grammar tyrant and established some strict guidelines for professionalizing the reports. These guidelines included the elimination of such words as "that", "which", and "aforementioned". Of course, there was push back and Mike was challenged with the Declaration of Independence. They asked if Mike would remove the word "that" from the document. Mike said yes and then quickly and angrily pointed out they had late reports needing attention but found it more productive to challenge the changes.

Apologies followed and work was accomplished. This showed the team Mike was going to hold them accountable for things. He had great integrity with his direction by not wavering on his instructions.

Mike was also consistent in his messaging of what needed to be done and when. He allowed them to complete the on-time work first, catch up on the late work, and continue handling the day-to-day operations.

The actions Mike took and leadership he showed in the development of his people started the repair of the trust triangle within the office. Not only did his constituents start to trust him and his leadership, they also found more trust in each other. Productivity increased for everyone and the level of professionalism grew.

HOW MIKE KNEW THE TRIANGLE WAS BUILT

Mike, being a leader, had people in the office he trusted. Relationships with them were built over time and respect of their opinions and observations mattered. John was one of the people Mike trusted the most. John was experienced in leadership and in the office. He worked with the previous bosses and saw how they destroyed the trust triangle with everyone.

About two or three months after Mike had established the rules and way forward, Mike invited John into a meeting. Mike asked John a simple question – "Are things better for everyone?" Mike believed they were, but needed to know for certain what he had established and done made a change for the better. John simply said, "Yes." And then John explained how the pieces of the trust triangle had been reestablished.

Consistency was the first leg of the triangle John discussed. He said the rest of the office was happy the instructions, directions, policies, and procedures did not change on a daily or weekly basis. Even more importantly, they did not change based on whether Mike was asked a question or one of the next level down leaders/managers were asked. There was a unified voice in leadership and it eliminated the previously experienced confusion. You see, Mike knew being consistent in his leadership and message would help everyone on the team achieve more and grow more.

Next John talked about accountability. He related how no one was really held accountable for work being accomplished or reports being submitted on time during the previous administration. And without accountability, work simply did not get completed.

John told Mike the accountability established boundaries and enforced guidelines everyone needed to follow. The accountability also tied into the consistency because it created much less confusion. Mike did not change from day to day or week to week, therefore, people knew what to expect. This made keeping people accountable and on the right path towards success much easier.

Lastly, John expressed how Mike's integrity for things had really transformed the office environment. Most importantly with integrity was Mike's open-door policy and willingness to answer the question of "why?" Now, keep in mind Mike was no pushover.

He always answered the "why" if it was to learn the reasoning behind a decision and to gain knowledge. However, a defiant "why" was met with strict and swift accountability…remember the Declaration of Independence challenge. This was a "why do we have to do it," not a "please explain the reason" incident.

SUMMARY OF A TURN AROUND

Mike knew the key to making the office great – Trust. He knew trust had to be built on the three pillars of Integrity, Consistency, and Accountability. Once these three things were in place, Mike knew everyone would become much more productive and successful. Mike also realized he could not conquer the challenge in a vacuum. He had to get everyone in agreement for the office's success. It did take time; but the transformation was amazing.

TRUST (LEADERSHIP) AND MICROMANAGEMENT

I don't think any discussion about trust would be complete without exploring micromanagement. If you are a person who micromanages their constituents, you (in my opinion) will never be a leader.

You can't REACH leadership because you LACK trust. I may hurt a few feelings with this statement and position; but if your feelings are hurt, I think you should take a good look at what you want to do and what you're really doing.

Key concepts to realize, at least in my mind are these: 1) Leadership is not management; and 2) Management is not leadership. I am a firm believer we manage projects, processes, and activities, but we lead people. This does not mean they don't overlap or interact. Leadership and management absolutely do work together. They are just different in what they do separately. Yet another reason why I believe a micromanager will never be a leader.

Leadership requires trust – trust by the leader and trust by those being led. I think a large portion of people who micromanage do so because somewhere in their existence trust was crushed by some individual, some event, or a combination of the two. This has resulted in a constant feeling of distrust. Distrust's friend is paranoia. And paranoia prevents any chance of trust existing in a micromanager's world.

Ronald Reagan is one of the people credited with the saying, "Trust, but verify." There is a lot to say for this philosophy and it is a good practice for us all. However, the micromanager forgets the "trust" part and only does the "verify" piece.

TRUST BUT VERIFY – OVERCOMING THE MICROMANAGER

I had a boss who would always say to me, "Trust, but verify." He did not trust and hid his inability to be an effective leader behind this phrase. I'm not saying one could never earn his trust; however, I am saying one could never really earn his trust for future activities.

Let me explain. Trust for this manager was built on the event taking place. Building a bank account of trust was not possible. If activity A happened and you did a good job, he had trust in you for activity A. As soon as activity B happened, you were back in the "trust, but verify" cycle. Once you did well in activity B and earned his trust, activity C would take place and the "trust, but verify" cycle would begin all over again. Enough successes did build a very small account for people, but if there was any slip in success, the trust account would drain (completely).

Here's an example I remember. (Please keep in mind there were multiple legs of the organization reporting to him and my division was not ever notified before he was notified.) One day the boss called me and wanted information about a situation people were working to resolve.

I asked him what he was talking about. He was a bit angry because I did not know what happened. He asked if my people had informed me of things and I told him no. He said I needed to get a handle on my people and find out what was being done about the situation. I realized I did not "need to get a handle on my people."

I knew if they were informed about a situation they were evaluating and assessing things and I would be notified by them when they had answers for me. You see, my people knew to notify me with more than a headline. Because a headline would only force me to ask questions they could not yet answer. This, in my mind, was a disconnect the micromanager had with everyone who worked for him. He wanted the resolution before anyone even knew what questions needed to be asked.

So, how did I overcome the obstacle of an untrusting micromanager? Quite frankly, it was through subtle, yet respectful, pushback. In the example above I simply asked him, "If others had informed him about the event, why did he have questions for me?"

I told him they should have provided him all the answers and if they didn't, I would need time for my people to assess the situation and be able to provide correct and complete answers. He did not like the response I gave him, but he could not argue with its logic, either. Ultimately, I always provided him the complete and correct answers, it just took time.

The other approach I employed was through ethical influence. This took time and a learning curve on my part. I would go to him with something needing to be corrected or fixed. At first, I would have solutions, but not documentation to support my solutions. I learned over time to have documentation supporting my position and pointing out the specifics of why I was right. This, over many interactions, started to build just a little trust, but not much in all reality. I was able to start influencing him by learning what he needed and wanted in order to get the resolution I wanted. It was not manipulative, just smart.

As I look back on the relationship, I never saw him as a "leader". I had respect for his position and to some extent for him as well. But, I saw him and treated him like a manager (a micromanager) and a boss.

The more I understood his position on things, the easier and simpler it was navigating the micromanagement. I just wish I could have figured out or received the information on why he had trust issues. However, I did learn from him, as I think we can all learn from everyone. I learned a lot of what not to do and not a lot of what to do.

Overall, micromanagement is a matter of trust, or lack thereof. When trust doesn't exist, leadership can't exist. The ability to make incredible things happen goes away without trust and without leadership.

This is why people call it micromanagement and not microleadership (I just made up a new word). Additionally, micromanagers think people shouldn't fail and work to prevent any failure from occurring. Sometimes they actually think they can achieve a zero-fail rate if they are "involved" enough. However, failure breeds growth and growth breeds better success.

TRUST AND ORGANIZATIONAL CULTURE

Trust, whether it exists or it doesn't, sets the tone for organizational culture. A strong trust triangle will allow for a strong and positive culture. Distrust will open the door to a weak and negative culture. I think a great way to determine whether or not trust is good in your organization is simple (I heard this from someone, but I can't remember from whom or when).

What are new employees being told about different departments, different employees, and different bosses in the organization? If trust between everyone is high, then the stories are positive and build instant trust and credibility with the new employee.

However, if they are negative, everyone needs to evaluate where the trust triangle has broken and work collectively to rebuild trust in the organization. I guarantee, if trust is low, the organization will fail. Trust is the key to success and the foundation of strong leadership.

CALL TO ACTION!

The call to action for you has duality. First, there is the call for the constituent. Then, there is the call for the leader. However, I want you to think about YOUR answer to each question from both perspectives. If you are a leader, how will your employees answer? If you are the employee, how will your boss answer?

THE EMPLOYEE PERSPECTIVE

1) What are you doing to build the trust of your leader in you?
2) What are you doing to build the trust of your co-workers in you?

3) What can your boss do to build your trust in him/her?

4) What can your co-workers do to build your trust in them?

5) Do you do things with integrity?

5) Are you accountable?

6) Are you consistent?

7) How can you help build a stronger trust triangle?

THE BOSS PERSPECTIVE

1) What are you doing to build the trust of your leader in you?

2) What are you doing to build the trust of your employees in you?

3) What can your boss do to build your trust in him/her?

4) What can your employees do to build your trust in them?

5) Do you do things with integrity?

5) Are you accountable?

6) Are you consistent?

7) How can you help build a stronger trust triangle?

Answering these questions may make you a bit uncomfortable (and I actually hope they do). But I believe it is important to answer each question and from each perspective. This should make you think a little deeper and a little longer for your answers. And remember, TRUST is the foundation of leadership.

Uncovering the Secret to Organizational Success

CHAPTER 2

TRUST IS THE GLUE OF LIFE. IT'S THE MOST ESSENTIAL INGREDIENT IN EFFECTIVE COMMUNICATION. IT IS THE FOUNDATIONAL PRINCIPLE THAT HOLDS ALL RELATIONSHIPS.

- Stephen Covey

Uncovering the Secret to Organizational Success

STRENGTH IN NUMBERS

- by Roscoe S. Houston

There I stood, waiting patiently for the front desk clerk to acknowledge me. She was giving me the cold shoulder. To be honest, I wasn't quite sure what I walked into. I was just greeted with a warm welcome filled with laughter and calming conversation with my new coworkers from a different department at the office just before stepping in.

This interaction confirmed that my shiny black shoes, beige slacks, and beige and black button up shirt were in full effect. It put me at ease to know they felt I was approachable but in few short minutes, everything changed. Now, I was on the other side of the door. It felt like I was in a different world as an unwelcomed visitor.

Finally, I received help from the front desk clerk who guided me to a seat so I could wait for my new supervisor, Ms. Katy Smith. About thirty minutes later, I heard the music of high heels walking quickly toward me on a mission. You would have thought it was ceramic tile flooring the way the sound transmitted off her heels as they trampled the carpet. She meant business, I thought.

SO IT BEGINS

The rest of my day went by in the blink of an eye. I met with Ms. Smith, and we chatted about a little bit of everything, except the obvious. Before leaving for the day, I understood the basics about where I would sit and some small projects that I was given to start with. In the midst of our discussion, it became quite clear that I walked into the perfect storm.

She was not just my new supervisor, but she was newly promoted from within the organization. That now explained the cold shoulder I got from the front desk clerk as I walked in earlier. Though Ms. Smith did not blatantly state it, she was tasked with helping to change the current culture of this department, and I was hired to help her. As the weeks progressed, I observed the way my coworkers responded to my supervisor and me.

Instead of allowing me to partner with the team immediately – who had already launched successful pilot programs before I got hired - I was left to myself to research and create a pilot program on my own. Unbeknownst to me I was pretty much asked to reinvent the wheel.

All the resources were already there, but it appeared that my supervisor didn't want to rock the boat, per se, and create a collaboration just yet. I wasn't properly introduced to my coworkers, nor were they told why I was brought on as a new employee or team member.

SILOS AND ISOLATION

I saw how the department worked in isolation and silos. Though we worked with one common cause, everyone had their agenda and they were rarely asked to contribute to significant decisions being executed on.

AN UNFORTUNATE COMMON THREAD OF MISTRUST

That was one common thread we all shared; we did not know where we stood with Ms. Smith or each other. She rarely spoke to us about our role and did not include us in significant decisions.

To break the ice, often I would go out and ask my coworkers specific questions to see their level of involvement. In response, they did not know or have an idea of what I was working on. Because Ms. Smith did not create inclusiveness at very pivotal moments when implementing new leadership in a fragile climate, it produced anxiety in the office. Inclusiveness would have afforded the opportunity to build working relationships.

A couple of weeks into the job, Ms. Smith gave me the task of developing, branding and leading the establishment of a new pilot program at a local high school. She did not provide me with a lot of support nor did she give me any guidelines on how I was to put this in place.

When it came to getting resources from my co-workers and other departments, it was up to me. Outside of the socially awkward moments of passive aggressive behavior and their subtle rejection, I did not have much interaction with my coworkers. While they told me they would help and support me, through their actions, I discerned differently. Often you could cut the tension with a knife. Their culture was tight and decisive, and I was not invited to become a part of it no matter how hard I tried to earn their trust. It was evident in their covert behavior.

I BELIEVED, EVEN WHEN NO ONE ELSE WOULD

They did not believe or trust me, so I had to firmly believe in myself and what I was hired to do. To do that, I had to be locked into the mission and vision of the organization; I had to be anchored by my Why. Why did I wake up in the morning, drive in rush hour traffic, and walk through those doors every day? Often when a negative culture has been in place for so long this essential component is missing from day to day work – it is easy to forget your Why.

My why was the basis for my journey to be a servant leader. I began to ask my coworkers how I could help them and be of service.

Also, I sought to learn more about their job duties and roles in the department. The more I came toward them ready to listen and engage, the more I watched the relationship change. My coworkers responded by providing support to me and the new pilot program I was developing from the ground up. They began to come to me before going to Ms. Smith, who soon began to pay attention to the relationships I was building.

It was important to me to report these interactions to Ms. Smith to maintain the trust we were developing and to keep her in the loop. The culture was shifting, and it started with my decision to have a heart of service. I could have followed the culture and continued my work in isolation with little to no input from my coworkers, but I would have cheated myself and the pilot program I was trying to build.

As we began to rally around each other for this common cause, it was clear that we were stronger together. I found strength in numbers. Through this experience I saw that no cares how much you know until they know how much you care. Having a heart of service is servant leadership at its best.

SERVANT LEADERSHIP AND TRUST

The philosophy of servant leadership originates from Robert. K. Greenleaf and is based on the idea that practicing servant leadership creates a healthy and caring environment by sharing power, putting the needs of others first, and helping people develop and perform as highly as possible.

It was amazing to see the difference in my relationship with my coworkers by modeling the philosophy of servant leadership. This experience gave me foresight as a leader. I was highly intuitive because I learned fast that leading from ambition or personal agenda always seemed to put the engine of the organization in neutral.

As a leader, I knew that we could not go anywhere without the engine. I saw firsthand how inspiring those around me was far more effective than aspiring to get things from them to get the goal accomplished. I found that getting them emotionally involved and engaging them at their level of expertise afforded me the opportunity to be resourced as needed for our common goal: Get this pilot program off the ground.

Though it was difficult, I became grateful for this experience because I was able to use what I learned in the next phase of the project. After developing and branding the pilot program, it was now time to take it to the local high school and implement it on the school site. I would stand again in a new culture with educational professionals and students who did not know who I was or what I was about.

When I met with the school administration, I walked into an unknown culture and atmosphere. As I observed the nuances of these new surroundings, I could not help but remember the methods I used to build relationships with my coworkers at the office.

I knew I had to take my time and not rush the implementation of the program or assume I had certain levels of trust that I had not yet earned. As the leader of this program, I had to start by building positive relationships with the administration and their students. This philosophy is also known as relational leadership. The idea is based on the premise that a leader who develops positive relationships within the organization or company is far more successful with bringing people together to attempt to accomplish change or achieve a common goal.

As much as the high school needed my expertise to start this program, I needed them to be engaged and resourceful as well. I made up my mind that if I was going to pilot this program successfully, the aim could not be to pitch the program as a one size fits everyone approach because every organization is fighting a different battle.

MY LEADERSHIP TRUST APPROACH

The first approach to relational leadership was establishing buy-in by getting and valuing the input of the school staff. I did not want to tell them what they needed; I sought to inspire them to share how this program would be beneficial for their school and culture. I did not want them to feel something was being done for them but rather with them. I began by developing an inclusive atmosphere by having meetings with administrators concerning the program to get their feedback.

Through our dialog, I tried to establish a space for ownership and shared goals. I made sure to discuss any mistakes or understandings that I may have had which gave them the freedom to do the same. I found that when ownership is established by leadership, others take on that same role and responsibility for their thoughts, aspirations, tasks, and ideas. It created a unified mindset which gives each person a piece of the program.

If there is something wrong with the program, "we" would fix it together, or when the program yielded positive results, "we" would share that success together. These conversations gave a voice to the administrators and included them in the purpose of what the program would establish with their students. I was there to build and serve, and I wanted to make that clear to everyone around me.

Once that was understood collectively, we agreed to delegate different tasks to whomever would take ownership of their ideas. Their shared decision-making and feedback put us on the same page and empowered everyone to become an active voice in carrying out the vision of the program.

I wanted to know their stake in the game and how this program could benefit them in the classroom and improve their interaction with their students.

They provided invaluable information that I could use to help me engage the students who would later participate in the program. My goals were not to create followers but to empower those around me to lead in their own way.

The students and program would be stronger with us working together, and it was important that I provide an opportunity for their investment in the program. A sign of strong leadership is being able to get people to say yes to your vision/goals when they have the option of saying no. What often happens is followers will say yes out of obligation and are forced to respect the title and position of a leader. This is called formal authority.

Respect is given not because it is earned but because it is thrust upon a person or a group based on title and position. A key element to building positive relationships is not only garnering formal authority but also informal authority. Informal authority is given based on earned respect - thus permitting someone, who may not have the title or pedigree, to lead people against the formal authority figures and institution.

FORMAL AND INFORMAL LEADERSHIP

The difference is subtle but extremely powerful. Strong leadership has both elements. As I built relationships at the school with the administrators and staff, I wanted to make sure the vision and goal for the program would be respected under my leadership. While I did not have the formal authority held by the Principal of the school, I had to assume informal leadership when it came to establishing and maintaining the program on the school site.

One of my first meetings was with the Director of Programs, Mr. Bradley Jones. I arrived at the school armed with the lessons of the servant and relational leadership that had successfully helped me navigate through office politics. I also began the process of using a tool that I would use for each meeting and conversation I would have on campus – it is a method I called "The Walkthrough".

THE WALKTHROUGH

The Walkthrough is a simple but effective way of getting an in-depth realization of the climate and culture you are walking into and how to use the information to bring the best out of everyone, accomplish goals, and achieve unity. The Walkthrough has three components: observation, active listening, and emotional intelligence.

I was able to identify what was promising about the school's culture. Also, I got a bird's eye view of what may appear as challenges and pressures on campus and in the community by observing the teacher-student relationships, peer to peer relationships, and staff interacting with one another.

My ability to observe these particulars permitted me to identify what needed to be elevated through a process of cultural excavation. The purpose of the Walkthrough is not to provide feedback or form an absolute opinion; it's about taking notice and forming a very surface understanding of the deeper issue I may or may not hear during my meetings with the Director of programs.

When I arrived at the school site, the ambiance was breathtaking. It was around lunchtime. The air was fresh and as I walked up the path of the school entrance - the sun pierced through the leaves onto my face providing a nice breeze.

LEADING BY OBSERVING

While I was on campus to meet with Mr. Jones, my observations began the moment I stepped on campus. As I entered the school, I was immediately drawn to the various student projects hanging very elegantly off the walls, encases, and ceilings. Viewing the completion of such artistry by their students showed me that school leadership valued teamwork. I continued the walkthrough down the hallway toward my meeting, and I saw students studying outside in the quad.

I thought to myself that it was a great way to learn and prepare for college. I had never seen a high school campus that was so intentional about building and creating an atmosphere designed to enhance and motivate their students to want to study in groups. I knew that I could take the culture the school built for student success and use those same attributes in the program for a smooth transition.

The Walkthrough was helping me to identify the learning environment that the students were accustomed to and I was able to see how I could simulate that into branding and piloting the program.

Even staff looked pleasant and happy with their working environment and coworkers as they were heading out to lunch together. Right before I walked into the meeting, I noticed that the school was very diverse. What intrigued me was many of the study groups in the quad consisted of students working with other students of the same ethnic background.

I knocked on Mr. Jones' office door and waited patiently for a response. He happily greeted me as I walked into his office. Part of the walkthrough is practicing emotional intelligence. It's not enough to be self-aware but being socially aware is just as important in developing and managing relationships.

Adhering to emotional intelligence, I knew what I said and did in those meetings would set a great starting point for building trust. I had to remain teachable by listening and making sure I was giving off good vibes. Everything starts at the top with leadership, and I knew if I modeled the atmosphere I sought to build in the program it would build confidence that I could replicate those same elements in the program.

As the conversation continued on, Mr. Jones became more transparent with me. Active listening provided an atmosphere of safety that made him feel that he could trust me. It sounds simple, but it can be really difficult to do well, because as I heard Mr. Jones speak of all the issues of seclusion in the student body, I had to refrain from providing the observations I gained from doing the Walkthrough on my way into his office.

I was intentional about providing a space for Mr. Jones to share his perspective purely based on his experience as the Director of Programs without him being influenced by my observations. Mr. Jones began to share with me about the unique nature of the school's population, which had students ranging from lower, middle, and upper class.

He discussed how many students felt intimidated and were not sure how to relate to each other. I observed these same issues during my Walkthrough on campus, but I did not share them just yet.

Again, my focus was to learn, listen, and help. Because getting his buy-in was crucial to garnering staff support on campus, it was important that I remained sensitive to how and when I would assert my position and what my program could do for the students, staff, and administration.

BUY IN AND TRUST

I looked for an invitation to share key information. I used a process called Informational Literacy to help me identify, locate, evaluate, and effectively use all the information I gathered through the Walkthrough to my advantage. After I continued to actively listen and receive Mr. Jones' perspective, he then opened the door for me to share by asking how I could help to change the climate on campus.

As leaders, there are times when we must make decisions quickly with little to no input from our team members - that comes with the weight and responsibility of leadership. These decisions do not build the relationship. Observing, active listening, and applying emotional intelligence fosters trust and mutual understanding. I began to match Mr. Jones' desire for student engagement and inclusiveness with the curriculum and learning models I would be using in the pilot program.

My words spoke to his goals of helping students from vastly different backgrounds come together to find common ground. I anchored my discussion of the program on my admiration of the model of teamwork shown by what I observed when I first walked on campus. I used the images of the school lay out, study groups, etc. to help me articulate how the program would align with the learning environment created on campus.

I assured Mr. Jones that the pilot program would only enhance the good work that he and his colleagues did on a day to day basis. Our conversation brought Mr. Jones to a place where he felt safe with me and the program that I would be implementing.

As our meeting continued, I discussed that we could use practical, real-world experiences that impact students on a daily basis. The program would provide a space for students to share their thoughts, fears, hopes, humor, and get support to work together through their high school experience. It would be a unique space for freedom and vulnerability. These topics uncover commonalities across cultural differences, bridging the gap between students and staff. I also noted that providing this kind of space for students could potentially open wounds, requiring me to utilize emotional intelligence and sensitivity when facilitating each discussion. I assured Mr. Jones that we would never let a student leave without closing up a wound that may have opened due to the nature of our conversations, and we would encourage other program participants to help in that effort.

If a student was triggered by a wound in their life, we would close it by creating a new perspective and a culture of empathy. The program would always leave on a good note providing optimism and goal setting for students.

By the time I finished my last word in our discussion, Mr. Jones had asked me to let him know when we will get started. I utilized the same methods in other meetings and conversations resulting in having the full support of the site administration and teaching staff.

This was not just a program I was spearheading in isolation, but they were willing to use their areas of expertise to support my leadership toward a successful program. We were stronger together.

After all of the leg work, the first day of the program had finally arrived. I knew I couldn't just push the program on the students, so I began to implement the same strategies that had gotten me this far in the process: servant and relational leadership, informal and formal authority, the Walkthrough, and informational literacy.

THE PRIORITY IS ALWAYS TRUST

It was a clean slate which meant building trust was the priority. Instead of dictating my position and what I would offer them from the program, I allowed the students to set the tone for the discussion. I met them at their level. We became equals regarding the respect we received in expressing our ideas and opinions.

The atmosphere we built dispelled the notion of attempting to exert control over the room or conversation. In bringing groups together where there is divisive tension, it's key not to allow people to "one-up" others.

Comparison is a barrier that had to be broken with adding value to each student through honor. I did not want to give them the impression that I knew what was best for them without getting their input or feedback on the real issues that affected their lives. It was a twofold process. As much as they were going to learn from me, I created a space for me to learn from them. It was important that we did that learning together.

How the groups were set up are just as important as well. I asked students if they would like to stay at their desk or create a circle and sit amongst each other. They agreed to sit in a circle, and I affirmed that decision by discussing how sitting in a circle benefits the group. This practice is known as Peace Circle Guidelines.

It allows everyone the opportunity to do the following: speak and listen from the heart, speak spontaneously, and with leniency, all while promoting confidentiality. This set the tone for us to develop and implement Ground Rules for the program. The ground rules governed our discussion and atmosphere.

We discussed elements of respect for differences. One of our ground rules prohibited cutting someone off when they were speaking. Anyone speaking was given the floor to be heard with respect, honor, and common decency.

I observed each student. I watched where they sat in the room, their participation, apprehension. I listened to what they shared, asked them what they wanted to get out of it, and got a lot of the topics from their shared interests and then empowered them to take ownership of those ideas.

To achieve the goal I set with Mr. Jones of finding common ground between the students in the program, I had to discover some areas of shared interest. Sometimes as a leader, we have to pull on whatever we can to motivate ourselves and our followers.

While strategizing my mind went back to the 1997 Chicago Bulls team. Though they were the reigning NBA champions, they were considered the underdog in the NBA Finals against the Utah Jazz led by Karl Malone and John Stockton. Despite the challenge before them, they had the chance to win it all in a deciding Game 6 in a best of 7 series. The Bulls were down with only seconds left in the game. Everyone thought the ball would go to Michael Jordan, but instead, he put the fate of the

Uncovering the Secret to Organizational Success

Championship on the shoulders of shooting guard, Steve Kerr, who nailed the three-point shot.

Although the whole world was shocked, Jordan was not surprised, and neither was his team. Both men had their differences, but earlier in the season were able to find personal common ground. Jordan's trust in Kerr was anchored by unlikely off-the-court similarities.

During practice, one season, Michael Jordan and Steve Kerr got into an altercation resulting in Michael punching Steve in the face. After tempers cooled, Head Coach Phil Jackson pulled Michael to the side and shared with him that he and Steve have a striking similarity: Both of their fathers had been murdered.

Upon realizing this news, Michael called Steve to apologize for striking him in the face. The bond they shared made them better friends and teammates.

I sought to create the same bond for my students. While they were so different, they shared many of the same experiences, and I sought to draw that out for them to see. I understood that building a program around topics that did not interest them would be wildly unsuccessful, so we spent the first meeting discussing a shared interest.

I asked them what they wanted to talk about and before long, our first discussion was about love, romantic relationships, and classes. Some students expressed their struggles with balancing romantic relationships and hanging out with their friends. Others shared their challenges with specific teachers or course work, and other students responded by offering help with the subject matter they had mastered.

I watched a bond form between students of different backgrounds. They identified shared experiences, excitement, frustration, and had some laughs, too. They began to look at each other differently. I saw that perhaps these bonds, if nurtured, could transcend beyond the confines of the walls that surrounded us and begin to seep out into their learning environment on campus.

Maybe, just maybe, when I walked out into the quad I might see one or two study groups contain students with different ethnic backgrounds instead of groups comfortably consisting of the same. I then asked them if this is a group they would like to have weekly meetings with and they replied yes. Then we spent the rest of our time determining the name of the group. I had a name in mind but held off to allow them to take part in the development process. Their participation created ownership and increased buy-in.

THE TRUST BUILDING PROCESS

Naming the pilot program was a huge part of branding. The name has crucial impacts such as setting yourself apart from others and creating confidences in a product you help create. Allowing shared decision making in the naming process produced a sense of direction and motivated those who took ownership of something they believed in because they had a say in creating the brand.

Which in turn allowed for the creation of brand ambassadors. When I explained the purpose of becoming brand ambassadors to the students, I elaborated on the importance of understanding reputation when wearing the logo of the brand on shirts and hats around the school campus.

I explained that reputation of being great brand ambassadors is keeping the ground rules in full affect outside of the four walls of our group meeting. I told them that being a brand ambassador was remaining loyal to each other and what we stood for, and that modeling the principles we developed together would entice other students to be a part of what we were building.

By contrast, I let them know we did not want others having a misunderstanding of who we were or what we represented. The same is true for employees and managers – we are a reflection of our place of business to those on the outside, and our conduct can potentially determine the amount of interest we receive from the outside world.

This allowed for students to be aware that they were a part of something bigger than themselves which only motivated them to return week after week. Through their loyalty to the ground rules set by the program, they helped us to maintain a positive reputation on campus. It also brought the mission, vision, and value of the program to others.

Collectively we were brand ambassadors that believed every student could benefit from this program and we knew that the only way of displaying that was making sure that we not only modeled our core beliefs but also saw the need to wear apparel that represented the brand of the program. I worked with the students to develop a plan that implemented a culture of inclusiveness throughout the school campus. As the student began to see the culture within the group change, they began to recruit others to join with little effort.

Students who came into the program more isolated and apprehensive were now empowered to invite other students and share their thoughts and ideas with the group. I watched them change before my eyes. These changes caught the eye of other students and staff who were intrigued.

Often other students approached program participants asking to be a part of the group based on these changes. It became evident that a good brand and model grows exponentially when it adds value to individuals as well as their community.

After hearing about the increase in student attendance, and better student/staff relationships on campus and about the atmosphere I developed in the program, my supervisor made time on her schedule to come to one of our meetings. She was kind but she began to assume a level of trust she had yet to earn. When I introduced my supervisor to the group, you could feel the distance the students created. Our usual snack was passed out as I gave the nod to Ms. Smith to have the floor. I stepped aside for my supervisor to walk in her formal authority as the overseer of the program, but the attention of the group began to wane.

Although a CEO may enjoy formal authority, they may not be able to develop strength in numbers due to the lack of influence which is an indication of lack of relationship. It was evident that the students felt the imbalance of power because of Ms. Smith's formal authority but together it was a sign that we built something stronger.

My supervisor got to see us open with our chant, go over the ground rules, and have the heart to heart talks about each student's day. We had a routine and structure down pat. During the discussion that my supervisor sat in on, she got to see how we handled conflict amongst each other when one student felt like he should be entitled to his peer's trust. Others joined in on the conversation showing empathy for his position of feeling alone and not having any friends, and sought to explain that no one is entitled to each other's trust. They continued to explain that sometimes it takes a while before others open up and how that process allows the trust to be battle proof, meaning earn over time vs. giving someone a responsibility that they haven't proven they could handle yet.

The student replied that they understand, and it was apparent they had never thought of it that way. The student thanked the group for the care they had given him, and committed to applying the feedback he had received. That conversation went well because of the honor, respect, and sense of belonging we created in making sure everyone was heard and understood. After the program ended for that day, my supervisor was impressed and told me how proud she was of me. I also thanked my supervisor for trusting me with the opportunity to pilot and brand my pilot program under her supervision. I am so glad I did not go it alone.

WHAT ARE YOU FACING?

As a leader, I am not sure what challenges are before you today. Perhaps you are a leader who has just come into a new organization/company and are tasked with turning things around?

Maybe you have been a leader in your organization/company for several years and are looking for a fresh vision and revitalization? Regardless of where you find yourself in leadership you will benefit immensely by implementing servant and relational leadership, evaluating your formal and informal authority, using the Walkthrough to gather information about the culture of your organization, anchoring your interactions with empathy, and reevaluating branding and collaboration.

By doing so you will become a better leader and establish a positive culture within your organization/company. It's all within your grasp and it starts with you.

Before ensuring that your employees or team members have a strong understanding of the organizational vision, however, you must ensure that the vision is embedded deeply within you. Your vision, or as I have referred to it as your "Why," anchors the course of action that you take within the organization and it sets the tone for your leadership.

I believe the only reason why most fail is that they don't write the vision and make it plain to garner and rally the support of those around them, and they give up too fast at the sight of pain. Having vision is having something to reach for, and it gives others something to be a part of.

Thereafter, you must come to one important realization – you cannot accomplish your vision alone. You can be the most amazing orator on the planet and have all the financial resources in the world. But your greatest strength is the people around you. Capitalize on how you utilize the expertise/knowledge each person has to provide. As you may recall early on in the chapter I could not jump right into the task at hand.

First I grappled with my "Why" which helped me to find a level of common ground with my colleagues and start the process of servant and relational leadership and buy in. It proved to be wise not to limit myself to one area for input. I found successful results when I took the time to build relationships with my colleagues to gauge their level of expertise which made them feel valued and added new perspectives to the work I was tasked with doing. It required me not to give up despite the obstacles that stood in my way.

I had to have tunnel vision. I persisted, despite being pushed out and discredited by my colleagues. I could not take it personal and neither can you. The work you have to achieve is so much bigger than you – it's about your shared goal and vision. You must weather the storm.

TRUST ALLOWS YOU TO FLY

Trust reminds me of the eagle. One of the most prolific and proud birds in the United States. Many associate the eagle with strong leadership and liberty. The eagle's reputation is anchored in their innate love for the storm. The eagle uses storm winds and clouds to help them rise above and position themselves to achieve their goal which is to catch their prey.

There is nothing more important than this goal, their very survival depends upon it. With tunnel vision, the eagle pursues its prey and uses all its resources (i.e. natural elements) to accomplish its goal. That is what leadership demands from us. Successful leadership does not seek shelter in its own wings but uses the force and strength from the elements around it to achieve its dreams. We must rely on the people around us. In order to do this, you must relinquish control. I had to rely on my coworkers, and later I depended upon the teaching staff and students in the program to provide the lift I needed to soar above the clouds.

The Walkthrough stabilized this effort and it can for you as well. You may find that you want to implement this process again and again throughout your tenure with the organization/company. One of the most frustrating disconnects between leaders and their followers is bad communication. Frequently bad communication is based on the failure of one party or both to apply active listening and emotional intelligence in conversation.

When this fails, you may find yourself leading based on assumptions instead of facts. That is where I drew the line with implementing the pilot program. I knew that I could not build informal authority and earn the trust of my colleagues, the staff on campus, or the students if I was not willing to listen to their perspectives. The Walkthrough, correctly applied, provides a space for that dialog.

I guarantee implementing these important areas in leadership will provide you with a happy and healthy culture and working environment. This model represents excellence, not perfection. No one is perfect but you will inspire everyone around you to be the best version of themselves.

Simultaneously, the mission and vision of what you are trying to accomplish will be pursued with a unified passion and enthusiasm. The pilot program impacted the students so positively, one of the students shared that he looked forward to Friday's not because of the weekend, but because he got to participate in the program (meetings were held every Friday).

The program was successful because we were stronger together. I implore you to no longer look for the strength to lead purely from within. I challenge you to find the strength in numbers. Leadership demands it and you will not regret it.

Uncovering the Secret to Organizational Success

CHAPTER 3

> **YOU MAY BE DECEIVED IF YOU TRUST TOO MUCH, BUT YOU WILL LIVE IN TORMENT IF YOU DO NOT TRUST ENOUGH.**
>
> *- Frank Crane*

THE POWER OF THE DETOUR

- by Joey Stutson

As leaders, it's easy to buy into the belief that we are an inherently untrusting society. For example, we all know there's no such thing as a free lunch, and will immediately question the motives of anyone trying to give us their services or products without asking for anything in return. Our initial thought is, "What's the catch?"

What's important to understand as leaders trying to uncover the secret code to organizational success is there is always a backstory to why an individual (or a team, for that matter) doesn't trust you and doesn't trust each other.

The story I'm going to share with you in this chapter illustrates how my humanity, and the detours I've experienced during my short life on this planet, affects my ability to trust.

THE DETOURS ARE REAL

You see, detours have been a steady part of my life for as long as I can remember (and even longer). In 1984, I was born with a birth certificate that stated my father as "unknown." I came into this world without a father and lived with my mother until age one, then with my grandparents until age eleven.

My mother regained custody of me at the age of eleven and I lived with her until I was fifteen, when I moved in with my uncle and aunt due to my step father being arrested for armed robbery. As a Junior in high school, my best friend's family invited me to live with them and they became my family. In 2003, I enlisted in the National Guard as an eighteen-year-old Junior in high school. By 2005, at the age of twenty-one, I was an infantry combat veteran.

At the age of twenty-three, I played football for the 2007 BCS National Championship football program. And by the time I graduated from Louisiana State University, I had marketed for the Army National Guard, worked as a Sheriff's Deputy S.W.A.T. team member, and graduated from Army Officer Candidate School.

MY FIRST DETOUR

My first real understanding of leadership through detours started when I returned from Iraq to marry my high school sweet heart. We soon gave birth to our first child at the age of twenty-one. Now we have six great kids all under the age of eleven.

I don't share this with you to win sympathy points, or to make you feel sorry for me. I share this with you because the *Trust Code* you're reading about right now can only be uncovered by understanding who a person really is, and what a person has truly experienced.

THE JOURNEY THROUGH DETOURS IS TO BE ENJOYED

In 2017, I discovered my purpose is much more than the intricate events and detours that led me to my current opportunities. In fact, everything I've done in life has been dependent upon how I responded to the detours in my life.

DETOURS BUILD TRUST

To my point, Charles Swindoll once said, "Life is 10% what happens to us, and 90% how we respond."

In my experience, there are detours that happen "to" us, "through" us, and "for" us. How we respond and lead ourselves through change, heartache, failure, and challenges determines our destinies.

This perspective is what allows us as leaders to uncover the *Trust Code* within our teams, within our departments, and within our organizations as a whole.

But have you ever reached a point of no return in your life after being faced with a detour? Something beyond your control that gripped the steering wheel of your life, waking you up to a reality you never planned? We all know this one: Someone or something causes a detour that affects our life trajectory. We did not deserve this type of detour, and yet it happened. We are left to respond to the new reality we never imagined.

Detour.

What about the detours that happen through you? You know, those are the types of scenarios we all play out in our minds, the ones we know we caused. Choices that sometimes haunt us and make us feel captive to the past. It could be a business we launched that years later, after investing all the work, sweat, and tears, the treasure turned out to not produce the results we envisioned.

Detour.

And finally, the detours I believe contribute to finding purpose and meaning in our leadership. The detours that happen "for" us. Learning to lead our lives and leverage these types of opportunities has been the passion of my life. The almost divine type of opportunities filled with mystery.

Are we really ready to embrace this type of detour? This type of detour is not about opportunities that happen "overnight," but rather an overnight opportunity that took a life time of preparation. A journey of unleashing the potential of your life to determine your detours or circumstances and whether they work for you.

When we, as leaders, are open to moments like these, the opportunity to enhance the trust of those on your team becomes palpable and tangible. It becomes real. When we're faced with those moments, those detours, and we choose to press into them rather than turn away, this is when real trust is developed.

For most of my life, I've tried to attain roles at work that were equal to my abilities. Yet, most of us desire a detour to save us from our current reality. We wait for the opportunity, hoping, dreaming, and believing more is available for our lives.

I believe you are right if you believe the latter statement to be true. Phillips Brooks wrote, "Do not pray for tasks equal to your powers. Pray for powers equal to your tasks! Then the doing of your work shall be no miracle. But you shall be a miracle." Regardless of what detour you may be facing in your life consider the giants who came before us like Norman Vincent Peale who wrote:

> "Change your thoughts and you change your world…Believe in yourself! Have faith in your abilities! Without a humble but reasonable confidence in your own powers you cannot be successful or happy."

The power of detours is about the inner drive to overcome extreme circumstances, to set yourself apart from everyone else, to be you, to be fully committed to pressing on and forgetting the obstacles that scare you from achieving your life goals.

If you are reading this and you are in a detour in your organization or business and you are trying to survive change, this chapter is for you.

Organizational change is the new reality we all live in. Reorganizations, mergers and acquisitions, workforce downsizing and expansion, the information age, socio-political changes and political issues that impact large numbers of people.

Our lives are filled with detours, and our responses impact not only our destinies, but our ability to strengthen trust within our organization.

THIS STORY IS PERSONAL

In my first leadership position, and for the first time in my life, I had to oversee a team of hundreds of volunteers for a large church with over seven thousand people attending weekend services.

I could not use a paycheck to influence them to work with excellence. In fact, I could not even use my influence to get them to show up. What I learned during these formative years of servant leadership is people want to have purpose and fulfillment at work, not just a paycheck.

There is more to our lives than just acquiring resources. I'll give you a snapshot of my story. I call it the "unknown factor."

THE UNKNOWN FACTOR

Not knowing who your father is means not knowing your medical history. Essentially not knowing your aunts, uncles, cousins, grandparents, and the list goes on. Today, a quarter of you readers will know this reality all too well. But what really hurt me growing up was not knowing my roots.

I was always moving, leaving, restarting, living in different households. I didn't realize my story was filled with so many detours until I was forced to stop moving.

I define the unknown factor as any void in life you do not know is affecting your life. You may not recognize it in the moment, but you could be causing your detours without even knowing it. Your detour might not be an unknown father, but it could be an unknown void in your life. We all face detours in one way or another. We are either walking into a detour, or walking out of one.

And the reality is these detours cause us to trust less. These voids in our lives strip away what little trust we had left in society, and we show up to the office with these same detours and these same voids. And they prevent us from leading at the level we were created to lead simply because who we really are never gets addressed.

For me, my reason for writing is to communicate to as many people as possible that detours cause pain, and pain gives us passion to fulfill our purpose in life. Understanding this one concept gives us the ability to build and strengthen trust within our organizations. So, in effect detours help us fulfill our purpose. Detours help us connect. Detours help us build relationships.

THE ROOT OF THE FRUIT

I love looking at trees. In southern California, we have some of the most beautiful landscapes: Mountains, oceans, valleys, and pathways covered by some of the most diverse and unique trees I've ever seen.

But what I appreciate most about the trees I see is the fact that no one can see the roots of the tree during its formative process. No one sees any fruit for years. In fact, some trees can take up to seven years before they bear any fruit. But fruit growing from healthy roots will last many years longer than fruit growing from a tree with unhealthy roots.

ROOTS TO NOURISH IN YOUR ORGANIZATION

As leaders trying to tap into and break the Trust Code, it's important to recognize how our own roots affect our lives. What's just below the surface affects how we perceive the actions of those around us. What's just below the surface affects how we respond to those on our team. What's just below the surface affects our ability to trust, as well as our ability to help others trust us.

It's too easy to focus on the fruit of the tree. We as leaders must remember that who we truly are affects how we act within our organizations. But here's the key: My detours have shaped my life, and the detours of those members of my team have shaped theirs.

The key to uncovering the secret to organizational success, then, is to simply take the time to understand our own detours, so we can better understand the detours of others. Building trust is the result of sharing our detours (like I have here), and letting others know how their detours, for better or for worse, have made them who they are.

STRENGTHS FROM DETOURS

Our detours make us who we are. Building organizational trust requires us to acknowledge this fact, and then embrace it. Ignoring our detours does nothing but break down our ability to help establish trust within our teams.

When we are coming out of any type of detour we must learn how to see the growth opportunities in hindsight. Often times we can see the vision of our futures when we look back in the rear-view mirror of milestones and events in our work. What we learn from the job transfers, firings, promotions, setbacks, boredom, and lack of purpose is what allows us to generate the relationships that lead to trust.

I will never forget how it felt to run onto the field of Tiger Stadium in 2006 when I was a member of the Louisiana State University football program. I was an emerging contender on the team and, as Jacob Hester said, "Sarge is running over people, he wants to play." I was on a life long journey and while deployed in Iraq from 2004-2005 dreamed of running down the field on the kick off team and running over the other team. It was my one ambition that I thought would heal the pain from my past. My unknown factor of not knowing my father haunted me. Here's the thing: In order to truly grow we must learn how to identify any constraints or pain from our detours. Not getting this one thing right prevents us from building trust.

CHAPTER 4

ADVERSITY CAUSES SOME MEN TO BREAK; OTHERS TO BREAK RECORDS.

- William Arthur Ward

ORGANIZATIONAL LIFEBLOOD

- by Dr. Stephen Kalaluhi

Trust is the lifeblood of an organization. Without trust, an organization cannot survive. Without trust, an organization cannot thrive. No place is trust more critical to success than in an organization that operates with remote team members. It's from this perspective I share my experiences.

I launched my consulting and coaching practice in 2014, and literally ran every component of the business. For more than three years, I wore at least seventeen different hats: I was the accountant, the marketing team, the administrative group, and the face of the company. I was responsible for selling, follow up, lead qualification, and lead generation. I was the payroll specialist and dealt with making sure client relationship management was taken care of.

LETTING GO IS HARD

The end of 2017 was the tipping point of my consulting practice. It was at this point in my business I made the decision to license my leadership frameworks and certification program to interested coaches and consultants, and committed to bringing on a team of certified trainers.

I was excited. I was apprehensive. And I was fearful. But what I dreaded most was the idea of having to let go. Every year since I first launched my practice, I would take possession of one word designed to align my overarching goals for the year.

My one word for 2018 was Structure. As 2017 came to a close, I knew the only way I was going to make a successful run at building a flourishing and thriving business was to create the structure needed to support massive growth.

Anyone who knows me knows I don't do anything small. So as I dreamed up what I wanted this business to look like, I imagined offices located throughout the nation. At first, having a nationwide vision pleased me. But then I thought about making an impact throughout the world. So I revised my dream to include offices located throughout the world, instead of just the nation.

I knew I had chosen the right word for 2018, because creating a global business on my own was not in the books. This realization forced me to start an informal search for men and women, who not only caught the vision I brought to the table, but whom I could trust with the business I spent the last four years of my life building.

Everyone in my life went through an imaginary interview that existed only in my head. My brothers, my sisters, my closest friends. Everyone I knew at church, those I had collaborated with in the past, even people that I had met only once or twice before.

It was someone in this last category that really caught my attention. He understood my vision, and took to the task of expanding it even further. This was the moment I knew I had found my structure guy.

NOT ALL RAINBOWS AND UNICORNS

I wish I could tell you that the last three months has been all rainbows and unicorns. I wish I could tell you the last three months has been one win after another.

Unfortunately, this is not the case. Here's the thing: the biggest challenge this company faces isn't found in our product or in our service. No, the biggest challenge this company faces is me. Specifically, me learning how to let go and trust those on my team.

TAKING MY OWN MEDICINE

As the CEO and Founder of a global leadership training company, sometimes I have to swallow my own medicine. We all know taking our own advice is tough, but when you're considered an expert in the field of Organizational Leadership, you have very little wiggle room when it comes to not leading well.

Fortunately for me, my vision for transforming the world through this vehicle that is leadership is so much bigger than my ego. This gives me the unique ability to stand in front of my team of leaders, and be as transparent and authentic as I can.

TRANSPARENT TO A FAULT

One of my officers told me transparency is great, but to be careful with how much I share. I agree, and there is wisdom in learning whom you can share with and whom you cannot share with. My goal is to surround myself with great people so I don't have to worry about those things.

Because here's the thing: I know organizational trust is the direct result of transparency. The way this translates in my head is, "The more transparent I am as a leader, the more my people will trust me." Will there be those who take the information I share and use it against me? Absolutely. But the risk of being this transparent is far less important to me than is the growth we'll experience as a company when I am an open book.

And by open book, I mean nothing is off limits. Literally, nothing. If one of my team members asks me a question, they receive an answer that is both blunt and straightforward.

No fluff. No beating around the bush. Just the truth, plainly and simply. And the best part about this approach? It builds trust.

TRANSPARENCY BUILDS TRUST

As a business owner, one of the things I've learned how to do really well is pivot. I don't have time to "wait something out" in the hopes it does well. If a program I create isn't received well, I pivot, change what needs to be changed, and get it back into my training rotation as quickly as possible.

I need everything I do to be a homerun, so I can continue to build out my legacy, positively affect leaders around the world, and lead this global leadership movement.

As a solopreneur, the only person I had to answer to when I made a pivot was me (and sometimes my wife…). As a business owner who is now responsible for the livelihood of more than three dozen trainers, I cannot make these decisions in a vacuum and expect everyone to just be onboard.

SHARING IS CARING

I share everything with my team. Everything I know, they know. I make a concerted effort to ensure they have every bit of information and knowledge I have so they can make great decisions for themselves and for their own practices.

When I pivot (and I do it more than most), not only am I upfront with what is going on, I am quick to explain the why behind the decision.

I take great pains to ensure my team of trainers knows my reasoning, understands my expectations, and is onboard with what the new pivot is, why it is better than the last iteration, and how it is going to benefit each of them as individual trainers.

Is what I share always easy to talk about? Absolutely not. Do the pivots I make sometimes negatively affect my trainers financially? Unfortunately, yes.

But because I am committed to being an ultra-transparent leader, I realize there are times when what I need to share isn't going to be popular, readily accepted, or even fully understood. My goal is to never let down any of my trainers. Sad to say I've let them down more than I've come through for them. But not a single trainer has come to me, publicly or privately, and said this isn't working out. Not a single trainer has come to me and said, "I want a refund on my registration." I believe it's the direct result of my transparency.

BUILD TRUST THROUGH TRANSPARENCY

Trust within an organization is one of those concepts that leaders know they need, but don't have a clue how to get. I believe this gap stems from an unhealthy focus on trust itself.

Let me explain: Trust is not the thing leaders should focus on simply because trust is the natural byproduct of doing certain other things well. This means the focus should be less on the trust within an organization, and more of those steps leaders must take to build the trust.

TRANSPARENCY RESULTS IN TRUST

The level of trust my team extends to me has little to do with me focusing on building trust. But because I understand the connection between transparency and trust, I focus on being as transparent as I possibly can.

This is where most leaders fail. They focus on the wrong things, get frustrated because nothing changes, and ultimately give up on their efforts to create change.

If the desire is to build trust, the focus must be on those actions and activities that precede trust being built.

TRUST AND LOSING WEIGHT

Building trust and losing weight are one in the same. Those who successfully lose weight don't focus on the scale. They focus on those actions and activities that result in the weight loss they desire. Looking at a scale and wondering why the pounds aren't coming off is an ineffective method for losing weight. Going to the gym and getting in a cardio session with a good mix of weight training, coupled with a steady diet of fruits, vegetables, and water, however, will move the needle on the scale in the right direction every time.

When the focus is on actions and activities that produce the results we expect to see, it almost becomes guaranteed we will achieve the goals we set out to achieve.

DEMYSTIFYING TRUST BUILDING

Transparency builds trust. But how? Very few leaders share everything with their teams. Very few leaders speak truth when they know the truth is going to be unpopular.

As a people, we are attuned to nuances and incongruencies in body language, shifts in facial expressions, and tones of voice. Most people refer to this as intuition, but there is an entire science dedicated to reading a human's body.

Even if we don't understand the science behind it, because we are as attuned to these things as we are, we can pick up on the slightest incongruencies and unconsciously know when someone isn't being as forthcoming as they should.

Even the best liars have tells. These tells create a lack of trust within teams, and because most don't understand what's going on, they simply walk away from an encounter with their leader feeling uneasy.

When the whole truth is not shared, the incongruencies in what is shared destroys what little trust exists to begin with.

How do leaders fix this? Simply be as transparent as you possibly can. Tell the truth, the whole truth, and nothing but the truth, no matter how hard or unpopular or angry those who hear it will become.

TRUST IS BUILT IN THE HARD SHARES

What I've witnessed since bringing on other coaches and consultants is trust is enhanced when I don't shy away from sharing with them my most challenging and defeating business-driven pivots.

It doesn't soften the blow at all. And I'm okay with this because my goal isn't to make this as comfortable for them as possible, my goal is to be as transparent as I possibly can.

What is built as a result of this level of transparency is a trust that allows me to pivot as often as I need to because my team knows my heart. They've heard me ask for forgiveness. They've seen me at my best, and they've witnessed me at my worst.

At the end of the day, I am fully committed to their growth, their financial freedom, and the attainment of their dreams. And until we figure this out and get this process dialed in, I will continue to pivot as often as I feel is necessary to achieve what we set out to achieve.

I TRUST THEM, TOO

My uber-transparent leadership style has built a team of trainers who trusts me to do what I think is best for them and for this company. The unexpected side-benefit is the realization that I can trust them when I pivot just as much as I hope they trust me.

This brings me to a great point: Trust is a two-way street. Building trust is a two-way street. The more transparent I become as a leader, the more my team trusts me. The more they trust me, the easier it becomes for me to pivot. The more I pivot, the more I trust their reactions are going to be positive, no matter how difficult the pivot is.

But the focus was never on building trust. It was on me being as transparent as I could be. Trust just happened to be the natural byproduct of my efforts to give my team everything they deserved from me as a leader.

If we're being honest, the world is full of leaders who have no business being in leadership roles.

Let's fix that by not focusing on building trust, but instead doing what we need to do to create trust as a byproduct of our committed efforts and focused attention on those things that result in trust.

Uncovering the Secret to Organizational Success

CHAPTER 5

Uncovering the Secret to Organizational Success

TRUE SUCCESS IS OVERCOMING THE FEAR OF BEING UNSUCCESSFUL.

- Paul Sweeney

FINAL THOUGHTS AND INSPIRATION

"Fresh activity is the only means of overcoming adversity."

- Johann Wolfgang von Goethe

This book was an experiment in bringing together seemingly unconnected leaders to give them an opportunity to share their stories about building trust. The result was so much more than I imagined it would be. Yes, only four authors are represented in this book. And in all transparency, we started with nine. The fact you are holding this book in your hands means these four authors are positively affecting the world in which they live. It means they have made an impact and are now affecting their legacy (and yours).

Here's the thing: These stories and examples are great. We've done some things that allow us to build and strengthen trust within organizations.

This means less to me than does you answering this question: "What are you going to do with this information?"

Without implementation and application, the information contained within these pages is worthless. These authors believe in you enough to put in countless hours writing, editing, and sharing what they believe will change your leadership life.

But if you don't do anything with this, we've failed to accomplish what we set out to accomplish.

So, I ask again. What will you do with this information? What will you change?

You have the opportunity to positively affect your world. You have the opportunity to make an impact on those you serve. You have the opportunity to take this material and be great.

Do not shy away from this responsibility. Do not take this call lightly. We firmly believe that the material shared within these pages has the potential to transform the world.

But we know that it must first start with you.

So go out, share this knowledge, and be the change your organization desperately needs!

Uncovering the Secret to Organizational Success

MEET THE AUTHORS

Uncovering the Secret to Organizational Success

BECOME THE LEADER YOUR PEOPLE DESERVE.

- Dr. Stephen Kalaluhi

Uncovering the Secret to Organizational Success

IN THE GREATEST OF HUMILITY

"The reward for humility and fear of the Lord is riches and honor and life."

- Proverbs 22:4

CHRISTOPHER DIEM

Passionate Leader, Christopher Diem is the CEO and Founder of the Carpe Diem Consulting Group, Inc., is the Vice President of US Markets and a Faculty Trainer for the StephenK Leadership Team, is a retired Marine Chief Warrant Officer 3, is a certified Project Management Professional, is a certified John Maxwell Team leadership trainer and coach, and is a certified keynote speaker. Christopher shares his story of leadership and how to implement the many lessons he has learned with business professionals, coaches, consultants, and people seeking more out of their leadership. He is driven to positively impact people, families, organizations, and communities.

JOEY STUTSON

Joey Stutson served with the U.S. Army during Operation Iraqi Freedom II in 2004-2005 as an Infantry soldier with the Louisiana 256 Tiger Brigade. Following his deployment, he played football for the 2007 B.C.S. L.S.U. National Championship team, and received an Army Officer Commission through Officer Candidate School. Worked in full-time ministry and marketplace experience as a General Manager of a $1,000,000 annual gross sales store. Currently, he is a part of the Ken Blanchard Company partnering with a world-class sales and consulting organization to unleash the potential and power of people and organizations for the greater good. An avid outdoor enthusiast and family man, Joey enjoys camping with his wife and six children in San Diego, California.

ROSCOE HOUSTON

Roscoe's life can be described with three words -- interdependent, resilient and creative. Roscoe believes a community cannot exist without unity -- and challenges anyone to try to spell it without you and I. To no surprise he wins that challenge every time! Roscoe is passionate about adding value to his life so that in turn he can add value to those around him. In 2015 became the first out of six siblings to graduate from a four-year institution majoring in Pre-Law Studies at National University where he learned the fundamentals of negotiations and alternative dispute resolutions.

As a Professional and Personal Development Consultant, Roscoe has become known for his strategic capabilities of finding solutions that help restore, and refocus company employees, products, and services back to a place of enhancing the value in what they were created to do. For Roscoe serving people never stops but it's how he serves them that sets him apart. Roscoe enjoys a challenge and is known for creating something out of nothing. Whether it's helping an entrepreneur find their niche or refocusing how a company articulates their brand and services Roscoe finds purpose in assisting others to execute theirs. Roscoe is married to Christine Houston; together they reside in San Diego with their two children Ezra and Zuri.

DR. STEPHEN KALALUHI

CEO and Founder of the StephenK Leadership Team, Dr. Stephen Kalaluhi is the creator of the Indispensable Lead Certification Program, FORBES Coaches Council Member, a certified John Maxwell Team leadership speaker, trainer, and coach, an adjunct professor in Ashford University's Forbes School of Business, a regular contributor for I Love Coaching Magazine, and author of *The Secret to Building High Performance Teams, The Crux of Leadership, CEILINGLESS, The Expert's Guide to Positive Conflict,* and *The Expert's Guide to Communicating Powerfully.* Dr. Kalaluhi helps leadership executives worldwide achieve levels of success not previously believed possible, and indirectly transforms organizations the world over through his ability to transform their corporate leaders. His passion is contagious and his drive is infectious. With more than 15 years of experience as an executive leader, and 6 years of experience as a Non-Commissioned Officer in the U.S. Army, Dr. Kalaluhi's heart for leaders is built upon the desire to see individuals intentionally and purposefully grow and develop, the desire to help individuals increase their capacity to succeed, and the understanding that individuals committed to their own personal and professional growth positively affect their businesses and organizations.

www.ingramcontent.com/pod-product-compliance
Lightning Source LLC
Chambersburg PA
CBHW070142230526
45471CB00002B/484